Draw It!

Aircraft

Patricia Walsh
Illustrations by Mark Adamic

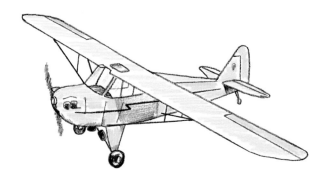

Heinemann Library
Chicago, Illinois

©2001 Reed Educational & Professional Publishing
Published by Heinemann Library,
an imprint of Reed Educational & Professional Publishing,
Chicago, Illinois

Customer Service 888-454-2279

Visit our website at www.heinemannlibrary.com

Designed by Meighan Depke
Illustrated by Mark Adamic
Photos by Kim Saar, p. 4; Mark Ferry, p. 5
Printed in China

05
10 9 8 7 6 5 4

Library of Congress Cataloging-in-Publication Data
Walsh, Patricia, 1951-
   Aircraft / by Patricia Walsh ; illustrations by Mark Adamic.
      p. cm. – (Draw it!)
   Includes index.
   Summary: Instructions and illustrations demonstrate how to draw eleven different airplanes and one helicopter.
   ISBN 1-57572-347-6 (lib. bdg.)
   1. Airplanes in art—Juvenile literature. 2. Drawing—Technique—Juvenile literature. [1. Airplanes in art. 2. Drawing—Technique.] I. Adamic, Mark, 1962- ill. II. Title.

NC825.A4 W35 2000
743'.8962913334—dc21

00-025665

Some words are shown in bold, **like this.** You can find out what they mean by looking in the glossary.

Contents

Introduction

Would you like to improve the pictures that you draw?

Well, you can! In this book, the artist has drawn some favorite aircraft. He has used lines and shapes to draw each picture in small, simple steps. Follow these steps and your picture will come together for you too.

Here is advice from the artist:

- Always draw lightly at first.

- Draw all the shapes and pieces in the right places.

- Pay attention to the spaces between the lines as well as the lines themselves.

- Add details and **shading** to finish your drawing.

- And finally, erase the lines you don't need.

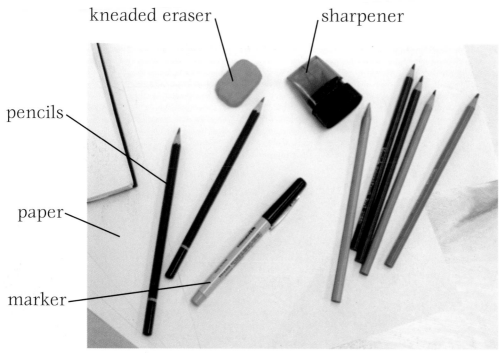

You only need a few supplies to get started.

There are just a few things you need for drawing:

- a pencil (medium or soft). You might also use a fine marker or pen to finish your drawing.
- a pencil sharpener
- paper
- an eraser. A **kneaded eraser** works best. It can be squeezed into small or odd shapes. This eraser can also make pencil lines lighter without erasing them.

Now, are you ready? Do you have everything?
Then turn the page and let's draw!

*The drawings in this book were done by Mark Adamic. Mark started out by **doodling** in elementary school. In college, he studied art and history. Now he works full time as an illustrator, but his hobby is drawing airplanes. Mark's favorite plane is the P-51 Mustang. His advice to anyone who wants to become an artist is, "Don't just draw your favorite thing. Draw everything, because that's the way you learn. Draw every day, and study other artists."*

Draw the Wright Flyer

The Wright Flyer was the first successful aircraft. Orville and Wilbur Wright experimented for years before building this flying machine. On December 17, 1903, at Kitty Hawk, North Carolina, Orville's first flight went about half the length of a soccer field.

1 Start with two long shapes that look like two popsicle sticks side by side. These are the main wings.

2 Draw two small ovals in front of the main wings. These are the forward wings. Draw two small, **vertical** rectangles side-by-side in the back. These are the **rudders.**

3 Join the top main wing to the top forward wing with two straight lines. Use short lines to join the rudders to the top main wing. Draw four lines below the wings and a cross line to connect the main wings to the forward wings.

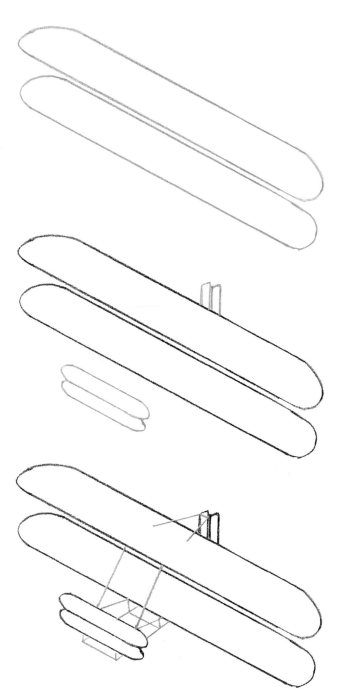

4 Connect the main wings to each other with nine short lines. Connect the forward wings with five short lines.

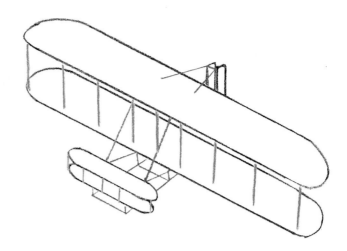

5 Add seven very short lines between the main wings. Draw a motor in the middle of one of the wings by making a square and **shading** it in. Draw a line along the top main wing.

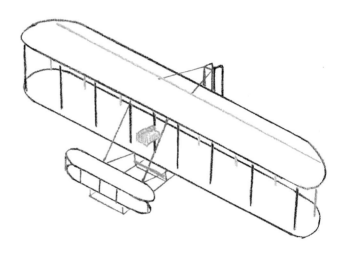

6 Add tiny triangles to show the tips of the propellers on the far side of the main wing. Draw curved lines on top of the main and forward wing. These are the ribs that stiffen the wings. Shade each lower wing.

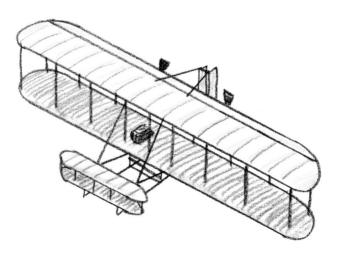

Draw a JN-4D Jenny

The JN-4D Jenny was used to train pilots during World War I. The instructor sat in the rear cockpit with most of the controls. The student sat in front.

1 Draw the body as a flattened oval with one pointed end. Add a narrow oval at the bottom left. Draw a short rectangular shape on the right side. Draw a circle at the wide, front end of the oval for the engine.

2 Add a long rectangle for the top wing. Make a notch in it over the **fuselage**. Draw half a rectangle for the **tailplane**, just above the bottom wing.

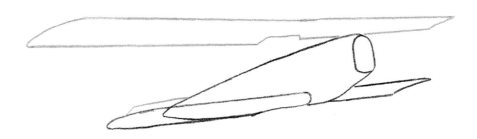

3 Add a half oval for the tail above the tailplane. Add circles for the wheels below the bottom wing. Draw half circles for two cockpits in the middle of the fuselage.

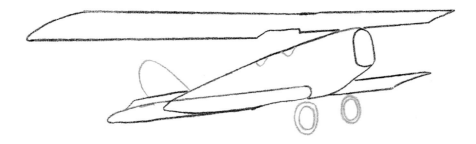

4 Connect the wheels to each other and to the plane with short, straight lines. Draw tiny half ovals for cockpit windshields. Make a slightly curved line along the bottom of the fuselage front to show the engine area.

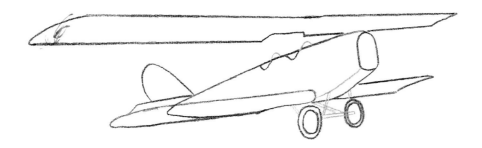

5 Draw **vertical** lines to join the top and bottom wings. Draw a line on the tail for the **rudder** and another line on the top wing for the flap. Add a line that looks like a backward capital L to the fuselage.

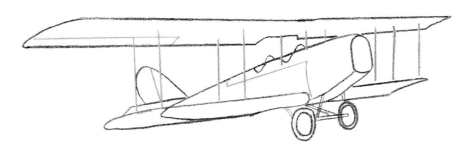

6 Make the first and last set of lines between the wings longer, so that they go through the wings on the top and finish in a loop on the bottom. Use narrow ovals to make a two-blade propeller. Add **shading** beneath the wings, in the middle of the fuselage, and around the propeller.

Draw the Spirit of St. Louis

In 1927, Charles A. Lindbergh was the first pilot to fly nonstop over the Atlantic Ocean from New York City to Paris, France. It took him 33 1/2 hours. He flew a Ryan **monoplane** named *Spirit of St. Louis.*

1 Draw a shape that is narrower at one end and wider at the other end. This is the **fuselage.**

2 Draw a rectangular wing on top of the fuselage. Draw a rectangular **tailplane** at the back.

3 Draw a half circle at the narrow end of the fuselage for the tail. Draw a curved line at the front for the engine. Draw the small tank on top of the wing. Add small rectangles for the wheel **fairings.** They hold the wheels in place.

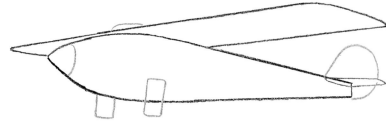

4 Add a chain of circles to the nose to make a motor. Draw circles below the fairings for the wheels. Divide the tail with a line to show the **rudder**.

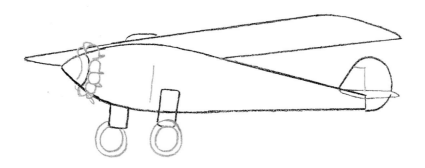

5 Draw double lines to connect the wings, wheel fairings, and the wheels to the fuselage. **Sketch** a few light lines to show the ribs on the fuselage. Draw a short line under the tail for the **landing skid.**

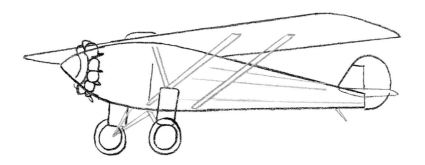

6 Draw a dark square on the side under the wing to add Lindbergh's window. Draw a line half the length of the left wing to add the wing flap. **Shade** the wheels and the area under the wing and tailplane. Write the name of the plane, *Spirit of St. Louis,* on the nose. Write its number, N-X-211, on the tail.

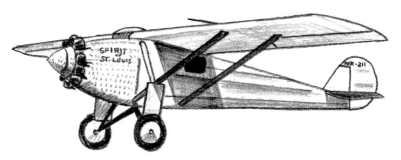

Draw a Douglas DC-3

The airlines wanted an airplane that could carry passengers comfortably, quickly, and cheaply, so the Douglas Aircraft Company designed the DC-3. It had 21 seats and began flying in 1936.

1 Draw a long, flat oval with one pointed end to begin the **fuselage**.

2 Draw the wing with two long, straight lines that begin at the middle of the oval. Connect the lines with a curve. Of course, there are two wings, but we can only see one in this drawing. Draw a small narrow oval near the end of the fuselage to add the horizontal **stabilizer**.

3 Add two fat tube-shaped engines on either side of the airplane body. Make a curved line at the tip of one of the engines. Draw a swooping curve, like a hill, for the tail section above the stabilizer.

4 Add the **cockpit** window to the nose.
Draw circles for wheels. Use straight
lines to connect the wheels to the body.
Add a little wheel under the tail, too.

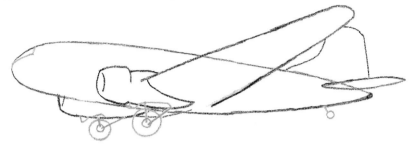

5 Draw a rectangle for the cockpit window. Make
curved lines near the front of the engines and
add small, dark squares to support the propellers.
Draw a straight line for the flap on the wing.
Divide the tail with a line to show the **rudder.**

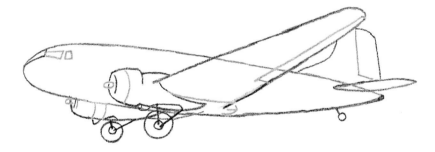

6 Draw three narrow propeller blades on the
near engine and just one blade on the far
engine. Add three passenger windows above
the engine and two doors, one in front and
one in back. Add **shading.**

Draw a Curtiss P-40 Warhawk

The Curtiss P-40 is one of the best-known fighter planes of World War II. It was flown by 28 different air forces. Its most famous pilots were the Flying Tigers. They were Americans who flew shark-mouthed P-40s for the Chinese.

1 Lightly **sketch** a long oval. Make the ends pointed to shape the **fuselage.** Draw two long half ovals at the middle to make the wings.

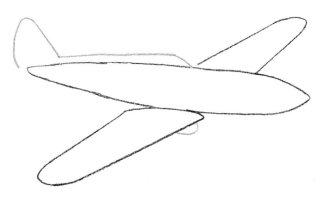

2 Draw a long line and the curved tail above the top of the fuselage. Add a small half circle to show the wheel **fairing** under the near wing.

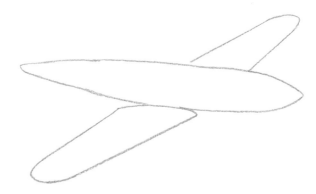

3 Sketch a curved line under the front of the fuselage. Use a short, curved line to connect the near wing to the fuselage. Add two half ovals on either side of the tail for the **tailplanes.**

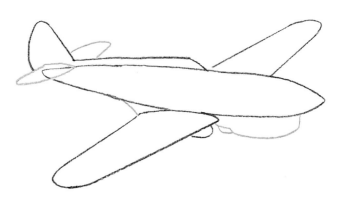

4 Add curved lines on top for the **canopy** and a C-shape on the nose. Draw a straight line from the canopy to the c-shape and curved lines where the wings attach to the body. Add a half circle below the nose and tiny circles along the fuselage.

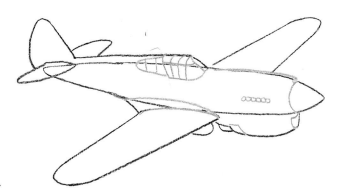

5 Add short straight lines on the tail, on each tailplane, and on each wing. Add a short **vertical** line behind the canopy for the antenna. Draw a line along the fuselage behind the nose to shape the top of the fuselage.

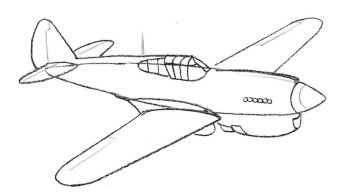

6 Draw three thin triangles to make the propeller blades on the nose. Add a shark mouth and an eye behind the propellers. **Shade** in the airplane, making the nose cone and propeller blades dark. Add shading under the tailplanes and above the wing.

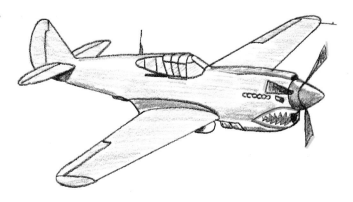

Draw a PBY Catalina

During World War II, the U.S. Navy's PBY Catalina Patrol seaplanes were painted black and called "Black Cats." At night, they slowly skimmed the ocean water and surprised enemy ships. In the daytime, they rescued crews and pilots from the ocean.

1 **Sketch** the **fuselage** with a straight line for the top and a curved line for the bottom. Connect the two lines. Notch out the lines on the top and bottom.

2 Draw a swooping line at the sharp end to make the tail. Draw two short curved lines on top of the fuselage to make the wing supports. Draw a wavy line along the bottom of the fuselage to shape the underside of the plane.

3 Draw rectangular wings on either side of the wing supports. Leave a gap in the middle for the engines. Add the **tailplanes** to the sides of the tail. Draw narrow ovals on the ends of the wings. These are floats that keep the wing tips out of the water.

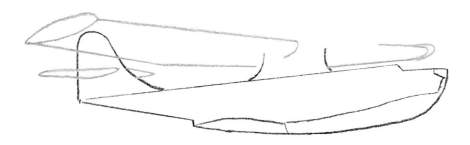

4 Draw two sets of **parallel** lines under the wing. Draw two oval engines between the wings. Make curved lines at the front of the engines.

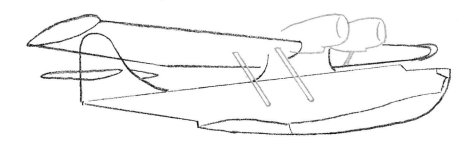

5 Divide the float on the near wing tip with a line. Add curved lines and a tiny oval to each engine. Draw a pilot's **canopy** under the engines and a gunner's window behind the nose. Draw a doughnut-shaped wheel between the parallel lines. Draw an egg-shape under the wing for the gunner's window.

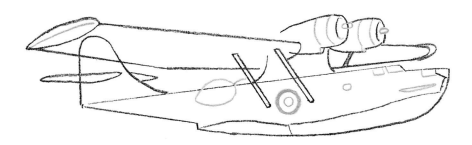

6 Add short lines to show the wing flap, the tail **rudder,** and the panes on the gunner's window. Draw three propeller blades on each engine. Erase the part of the tail that is behind the wing and add **shading** beneath the wing, under the tailplane, and below the fuselage.

Draw a Piper J-3 Cub

William T. Piper thought people wanted to have their own small planes. So he had the Piper J-3 Cub built in 1938. Piper was right. His airplanes were so popular that the name Cub became a nickname for all light planes.

1 Draw an oval pointed at one end for the body. Add a curved triangle to the pointed end for the tail.

2 Draw a long rectangle with rounded corners on top for the main wing. Add two small half ovals on either side of the tail.

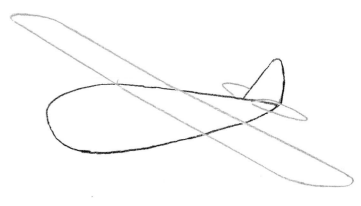

3 Draw a box and a triangle next to each other for the **cockpit.** Make a curved line that runs from the cockpit to the front of the nose. Under the airplane draw two lines that don't quite meet to begin the landing gear.

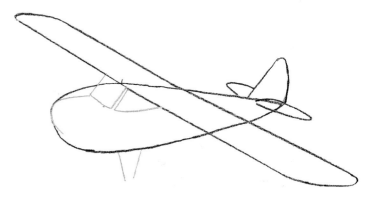

4 Add two circles for wheels. Make a rectangle on top of the wing just above the cockpit. Draw a curved line inside the cockpit for the instrument panel. Add a very small wheel beneath the tail of the plane.

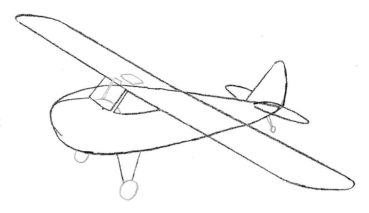

5 Add small circles on the side of the nose for the engine. Draw lines between the wheels and two long lines to connect each wing to the body. Add two short lines near the cockpit for the door. Draw a circle on the end of the nose.

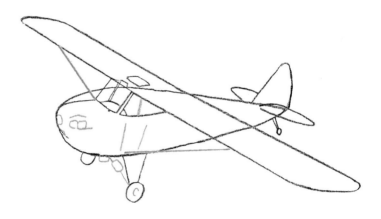

6 Add two short lines under each wing to connect the wings and the body. **Shade** a rectangle on the tip of the nose for the propeller. Add a line to the back edge of each wing for flaps. Divide the tail with a line for the **rudder.** Draw a lightning bolt stripe along the side of the plane. Add more shading along the body, under the wing.

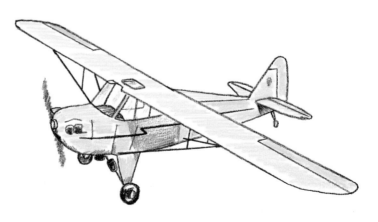

Draw a C-130 Hercules

The C-130 Hercules has been flying in peacetime and war since 1956. It airlifts food and medicine to people all over the world, and it fights forest fires. The C-130 also carries soldiers and paratroopers to wherever they are needed.

1 Draw a tube shape for the body. Add long, straight lines to the front of the body to begin the main wings. Add shorter lines at the back for the **tailplane.**

2 Finish the wings and the tailplane by drawing and connecting them to another set of slightly curved lines.

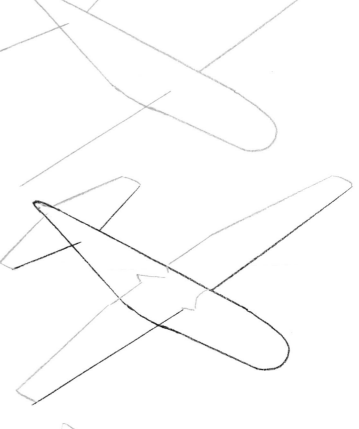

3 Add a triangle shape with the tip cut off to the pointed end of the body. Draw an oval under the near wing. This is for the landing gear. There is landing gear under the far wing, but it cannot be seen in this picture.

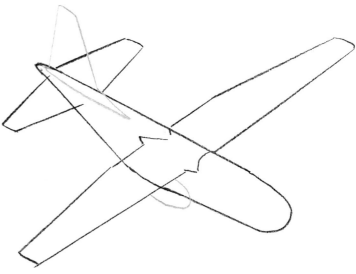

4 Draw four ovals in front of the wings for the **turboprop** engines. Make tiny ovals at the end of each one. Add two curved lines, front and midway, on the body of the airplane.

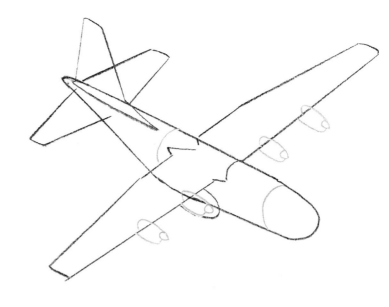

5 Make two lines for the flaps on each wing and each tailplane. Divide the tail with a line to show the **rudder.** Draw a small oval under each wing between the engines. Draw a circle on the nose.

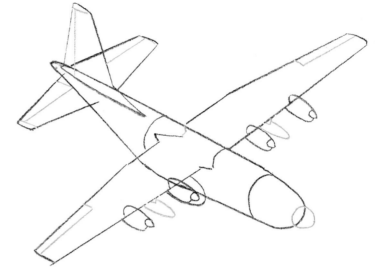

6 Finish your drawing with little windows above the nose. Make three dots for windows along the side. Show spinning propellers by drawing a circle in front of each engine. **Shade** in the nose, and add shading or color to the airplane body, the wing tips, tailplanes, and tail.

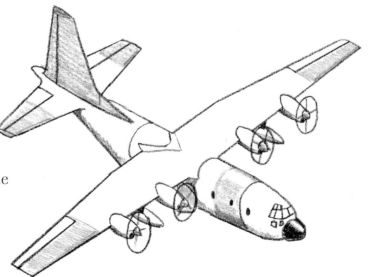

Draw a Learjet

The small, fast Learjet made its first flight in 1963. It set a record in 1965 when it flew **round trip** from Los Angeles to New York and back in 11 hours, 36 minutes. The Learjet is popular with businesses that want to own their own aircraft.

1 Draw a flat oval that is pointed at both ends. Add a small rectangle for the far wing and two **parallel** lines for the near wing.

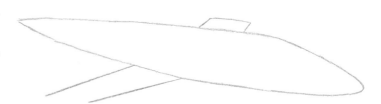

2 Reshape the nose by drawing a downward slanting line at the front of the plane. Erase the extra line above. Draw the tail. The top and back are like a rectangle, but the front slopes away. Make a line above the near wing.

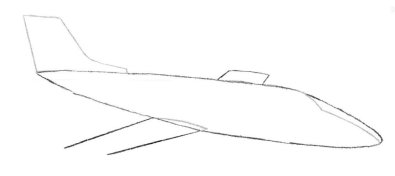

3 Add long ovals to the end of each wing. These are the wing tanks.

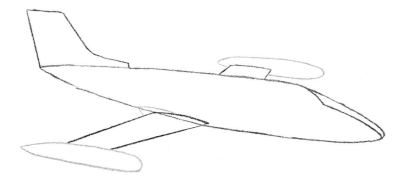

Add the **tailplanes.** These look like little wings near the top of the tail. Draw an oval for the engine behind the near wing. Draw just the top of the engine behind the far wing. Add a very small triangle shape under the tail.

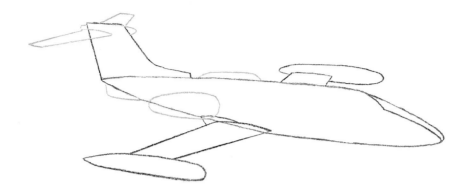

 Draw a **vertical** line on the tail for the **rudder.** Add curved lines near the front and the back of the engines and wing tanks. Add a small curved line to the nose, too. Draw short straight lines on the wings.

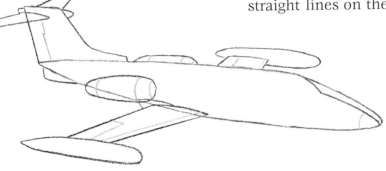

 Draw the pilot's curved **cockpit** window and two round side windows. Leave some white in the windows to make them look like glass. Add **shading** below the tailplanes and along the bottom of the plane. Shade or color in the tips of the wing tanks and the nose.

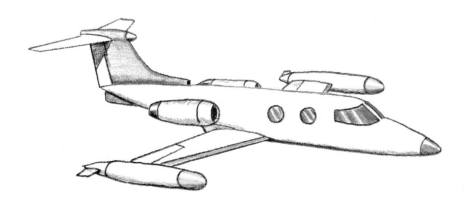

Draw a Boeing 747

The Boeing 747 is the world's largest passenger airplane. It first flew in 1969. It can fly farther than any other airliner and carry as many as 600 passengers. *Air Force One*, the airplane of the president of the United States, is a 747.

1 Draw a long oval shape. Make the top straight with a bump at the front. Make the bottom more curved and narrower in the back.

2 Draw an oval on the side of the **fuselage**.

3 Add the wings. The far wing appears near the center of the plane. The near wing is drawn closer to the front.

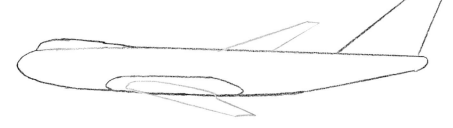

Make one **tailplane** by drawing a shape like a 7 just behind the tail. Draw a rectangle for the other tailplane below the tail. Draw two rectangles under the near wing. This is where the engines will attach.

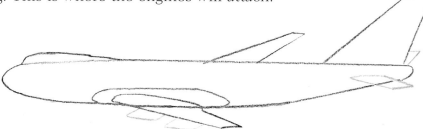

Draw two engines under the near wing. Each engine has two sections. Each section has rounded corners. There are two more engines under the far wing, but they cannot be seen.

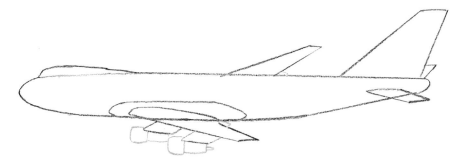

Add small circles for the pilot's windows and larger ovals for five cabin doors. Make dots for the cabin windows for the passengers. On the narrow end of the aircraft, draw a large shape like a triangle with the tip cut off. This is the tail. Draw a straight line on the tail for the flap. Add **shading** under the wings. Then color the 747 with the colors of your favorite airline.

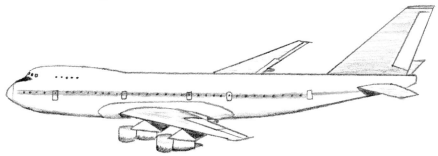

Draw an F-15 Eagle

The first F–15 Eagle took its **maiden flight** in 1972 and continues to serve as the fighter of the U.S. Air Force. It can find, track, and attack enemy aircraft. It can engage in air combat and turn sharply without losing airspeed.

1 **Sketch** three overlapping oval shapes for the body. Draw the large one first, then the medium, then the small one.

2 Draw rectangular shapes to make a wing on each side and two tails behind the body.

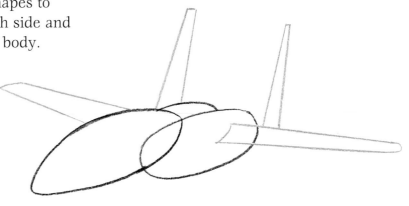

3 Draw a shape like a curved Y in the center of the medium oval. Erase the front of this oval and, in its place, draw a square for the jet intake. Draw a line along the back edge of each wing. Add a small circle to the tip of each tail.

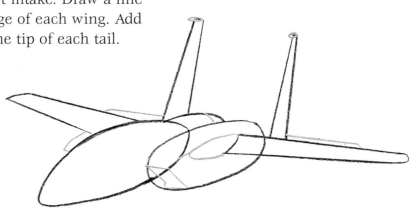

Add a half circle for the pilot's **canopy**. Add a shape like a backward C on the pointed end to make the nose cone. Draw short lines to make the panels on the jet intake.

Draw half circles on the canopy. Then draw a rectangle inside the canopy for the pilot's seat. Draw a small triangle to extend the tail under the wing.

Draw a half circle on the tip of the nose. Add a **vertical** line under the nose for the antenna. **Shade** the area directly under the wing and inside the jet intake.

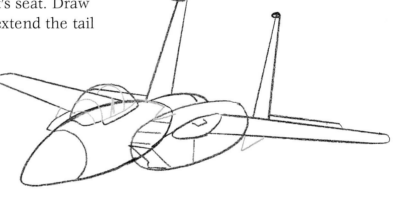

Draw a Bell JetRanger Helicopter

The Bell JetRanger is a popular helicopter. It is used in police work and as an ambulance. It is also used by radio and TV stations to gather information for news and traffic reports.

1 **Sketch** an oval for the body. Draw two nearly **parallel** lines from the back. This is the **boom.**

2 Add two rectangles to the end of the boom. Draw a straight line along the top of the boom to connect it to the body of the aircraft. Draw a shape like a flat circle on top of the helicopter.

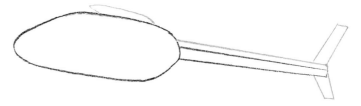

3 Erase the front of the oval and reshape it with a slanted line. Draw a triangle for the pilot's window and two rectangles for side windows. Add two **vertical** lines on top for the **rotor** post. Add a short curved line near the top of the oval to shape the **fuselage.**

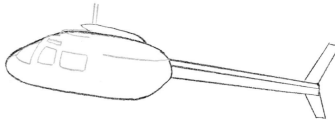

Draw a cross bar on top of the rotor post. Add two bumps to the top of the body for exhaust stacks. Add a rectangle to the center of the boom.

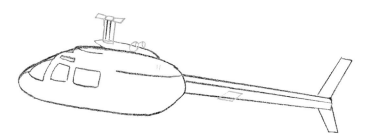

 Draw two narrow, long triangles on top of the rotor post to make the helicopter blades. Draw two triangles on the end of the boom to make the tail rotor.

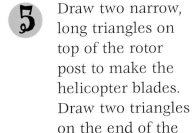

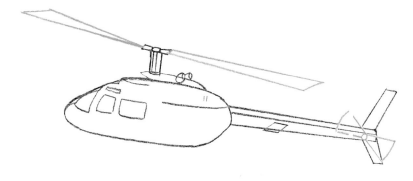

Draw two rectangles around each side window to make the doors. Draw two short curved lines under the helicopter. Connect them with a straight line. **Shade** the rotor blades, the windows, and the underside. Add color or shading to the tail rotor and the body of the helicopter.

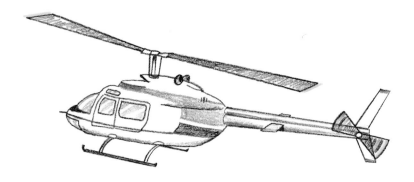

Glossary

boom long pole or beam

canopy sliding cover over the place in an airplane where the pilot sits

cockpit place where the pilot sits in an airplane

doodling making little drawings at the edges of paper; cartooning

fairing outer covering that reduces air resistance

fuselage main body of the aircraft

landing skid runner on the bottom of an aircraft that allows it to slide when landing

maiden flight first flight

monoplane aircraft with one set of wings

rotor system of circling blades that enables a helicopter to fly

round trip traveling to a place and then back again

rudder flat piece of wood or metal at the rear end of an aircraft that is used for steering

stabilizer device for keeping an aircraft steady

tailplane tail including all the flat pieces of wood or metal at the rear end of the plane that are used for steering

turboprop engine that uses both a propeller and exhaust gases for thrust

Art Glossary

guideline
light line, used to shape a drawing, that is usually erased in the final drawing

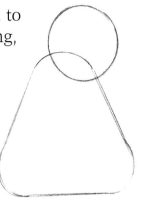

kneaded eraser
soft, squeezable eraser used to soften dark pencil lines

parallel
straight lines that lie next to one another, but never touch

shade
make darker than the rest

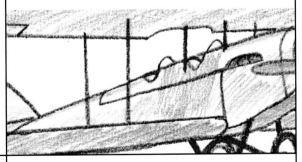

sketch
draw quickly and roughly

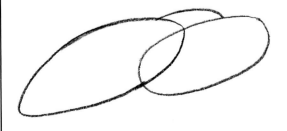

vertical
straight up and down

More Books

Books about Drawing

Ames, Lee J. *Draw 50 Airplanes, Aircraft, and Spacecraft.* Madison, Wis.: Demco Media, 1977.

McKee, Karen A. *How to Draw Airplanes.* New York: Kidsbooks, Inc., 1990.

Books about Aircraft

Armentrout, Patricia. *Extreme Machines. . .in the Air.* Vero Beach, Fla.: Rourke, Inc., 1998.

Graham, Ian. *Aircraft.* Austin, Tex.: Raintree Steck-Vaughn Publishers, 1999.

Manning, Gerry. *One Thousand Airlines in Color.* Stillwater, Minn.: Voyageur Press, 1998.

Index